HOW TO REVISE...

...and remember.

Martin Williams Bsc, MA

foulsham

LONDON · NEW YORK · TORONTO · SYDNEY

foulsham

Yeovil Road, Slough, Berkshire, SL1 4JH

ISBN 0 - 572 - 01862 - 2

Printed in Great Britain
at Maple Press (U.K)Ltd, Slough

HOW TO REVISE

Contents

Section 1	Passing Your Exams	4
Section 2	Making Notes	5
Section 3	Different Ways of Making Notes	6
Section 4	Pattern Notes	8
	Examples of Pattern Notes	9
	Students' Comments on Example Pattern Notes	12
	More Comments on Pattern Notes	13
Section 5	Summary Notes	14
Section 6	Efficient Reading	16
	SQ3R Method	17
Section 7	Writing Essays	18
Section 8	Revision	22
	Memory Test	24
Section 9	Organising Your Work	25
	Your Revision Plan	27
	Some More Revision Rules	34
	Now You Are Organised,What Next?	36
Section 10	On the Exam Day	37
	Something Extra	39
	Answers to Memory Tests	40

SECTION 1 PASSING YOUR EXAMS

TO PASS YOUR EXAMS, YOU NEED:

1 to have done the work that the exam is testing;

2 to understand what you have learned;

3 to remember it and have it securely in your head when you come to the exam.

THIS BOOK WILL HELP YOU:

1 to identify the most important parts of your work that must be remembered;

2 to revise efficiently so that you understand and remember;

3 to prepare yourself for the exam.

YOU WILL LEARN:

1 why making notes is so useful to you;

2 how to make notes that include the essential material — that which you must know;

3 how to make efficient notes that are easy to remember;

4 how to use your reading time effectively;

5 how to write well-planned essays;

6 how to plan, organise and do your revision. All adding up to

EXAM SUCCESS!

MAKING NOTES

SECTION 2

WHY MAKE NOTES?

- to help you remember;
- to be a personal record;
- to aid understanding;
- to learn more effectively;
- to aid homework essays, questions, answering, planning, and talks;
- for revision for exams.

WHY ARE EFFICIENT NOTES IMPORTANT?

Any form of note making increases your chances of remembering things by six times, but if you make notes in the special and effective way this book shows you it can improve your chances of remembering things by up to 100 times!

BAD NOTES ARE UNHELPFUL IF THEY:

- are illegible and you can't read them;
- have too much noted down — you can't take it all in or find things quickly;
- are whole passages quoted from books. The important bits won't be highlighted;
- are boring. You won't bother reading them;
- are untidy. You will find it difficult to find the information you need;
- aren't organised. You won't see how things link up;
- are never looked at again.

GOOD NOTES WILL HELP YOU BY:

- showing what is important and what can be ignored;
- helping you to see how things are linked together;
- putting things into groups where they belong;
- making you ask new questions;
- having the ideas put down in your own words;
- being set out clearly so you can find things quickly;
- allowing you to add things easily in the right place;
- copying the shape of things as your brain sees it;
- being good to look at and memorable.

SECTION 3 DIFFERENT WAYS OF MAKING NOTES

You can make:

LINEAR NOTES

These are written line by line, as in a book. They can be whole sentences or shortened sentences.

Or you can make:

PATTERN NOTES

These have the main subject in the centre and notes about it are written around it. A pattern rather like a map is made.

Or you can make:

SUMMARY NOTES

These are another form of pattern notes, that look a bit similar to linear notes.

Linear notes Disadvantages

- Only 10 words out of 100 will be the important ones.
- You have to waste time reading the other 90 words.
- Revising big blocks of text is boring and difficult.

Linear notes Advantages

- We are used to reading lines when we read books.
- Lines are familiar and it may be hard to get used to a different style of notes.

Here is an example of one girl's linear notes.

Nerves Each muscle has a nerve messages go down. Messages pass over cerebrium down spinal cord to motor neurones. At end nerve endings there is a motor endplate and cerebrium (of brain) reieives from sense organ and controls muscle movement. Two types of muscle are voluntary muscle, and involuntary muscle. Voluntary muscle needs nervous stimulus (decide whether to or not). Involemtary just happens don't think about it (inter costal muscles, diaphragm (diaphragm can be controled by you when running)

These are pattern notes

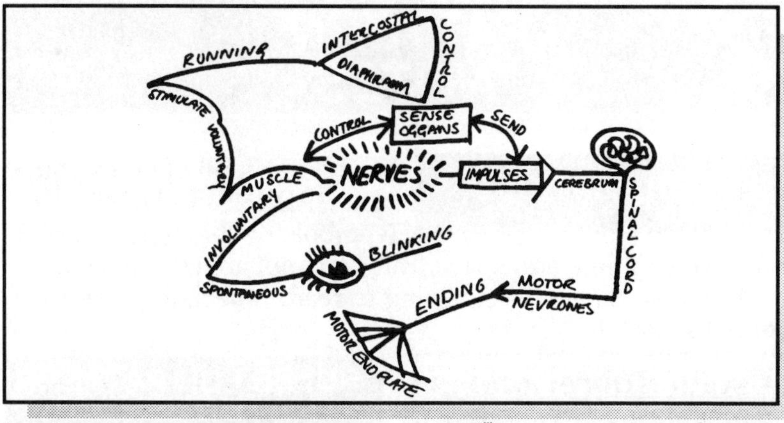

Pattern notes Disadvantages:

- If they are untidy they will be difficult to remember.
- If there's too much information, they may be hard to take in.
- If the pattern is complicated you may spend ages working out what you meant.

Pattern notes Advantages

- You only need write down the important points.
- You can easily show how things link up.
- All the information you need is on one page.
- When you have made a pattern, your brain will remember the whole shape of the topic.

This is part of a page of summary notes

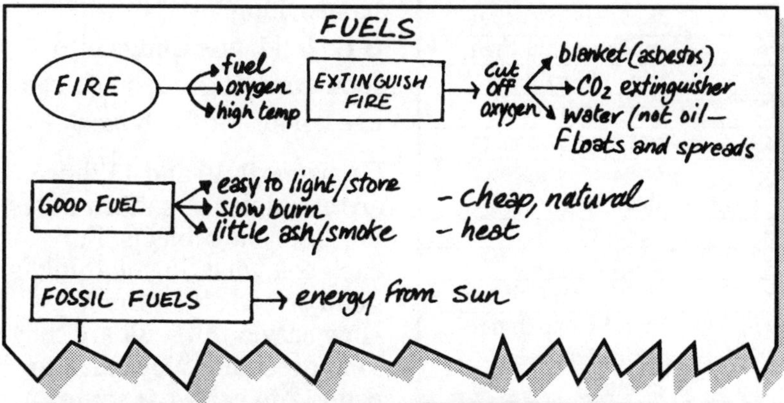

The most useful notes are PATTERN NOTES page 8 and SUMMARY NOTES page 14.

SECTION 4 PATTERN NOTES

ABBREVIATIONS

Whichever kind of notes you make, ABBREVIATIONS (symbols or shortened words) will save you time and space. But don't put abbreviations on work that someone else is going to read, especially if they are going to mark it.

Useful Abbreviations

cf	compare (with)
e.g.	for example
etc.	et cetera; and so on
et al	and others
ibid.	in the same place (in a book or article)
i.e.	that is
N.B.	note well (something important)
viz.	namely (naming someone or something you have referred to)
∴	therefore; thus; so
∵	because
=	is equal to; the same as
≠	is not equal to; not the same as
+	plus; and more
−	minus; less
>	greater than
<	less than
≫	much greater than
≪	much less than
∝	proportional to
∝̸	not proportional to
≧	equal to or greater than
%	per cent
÷	divide; divided by
x	multiply; multiplied by
/	insert (something which has been omitted)
→	from....to; leads to; results in

RULES FOR PATTERN NOTES

1 Divide the information into a few main topics;
2 Only write down what is important;
3 Link things that go together;
4 Write on one side of the line, one or two words only before line changes direction.
5 small letters or CAPITALS for topic headings;
6The TITLE should be in a central box in capitals;
7 Print in small letters or CAPITALS to makes it clear. Don't use normal handwriting.
8 Be bold: box things into their correct groups.You can use colour for the boxes.

On pages 9, 10 and 11 there are examples of pattern notes for different subjects. For each set, what do you think is good or bad about them? How easy or difficult are they to understand? Now, turn to page 12 to see what some other students thought about them.

EXAMPLES OF PATTERN NOTES

Example A: a year eight student's notes

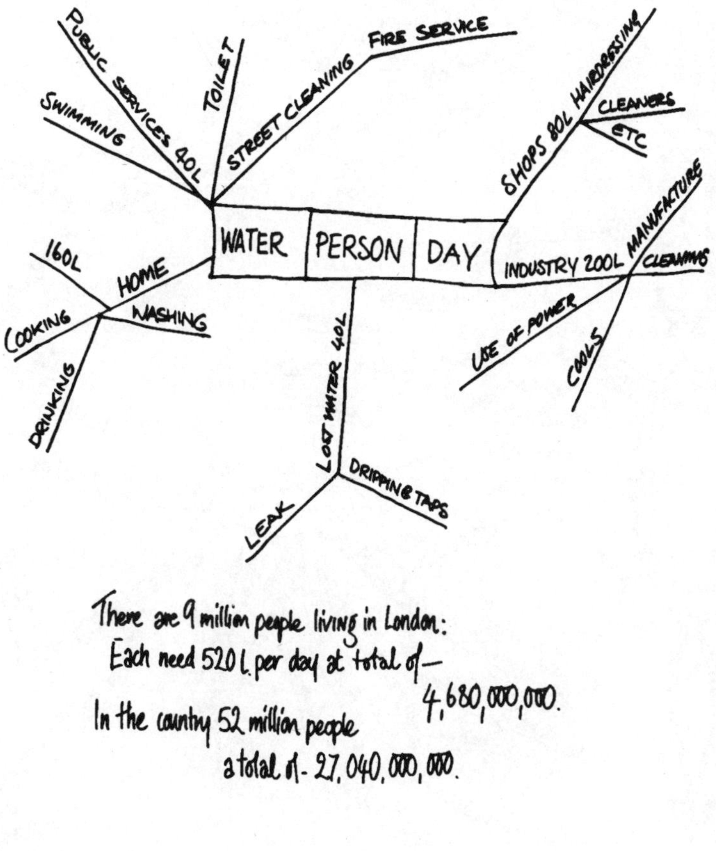

EXAMPLES OF PATTERN NOTES

Example B: a year eleven student's notes

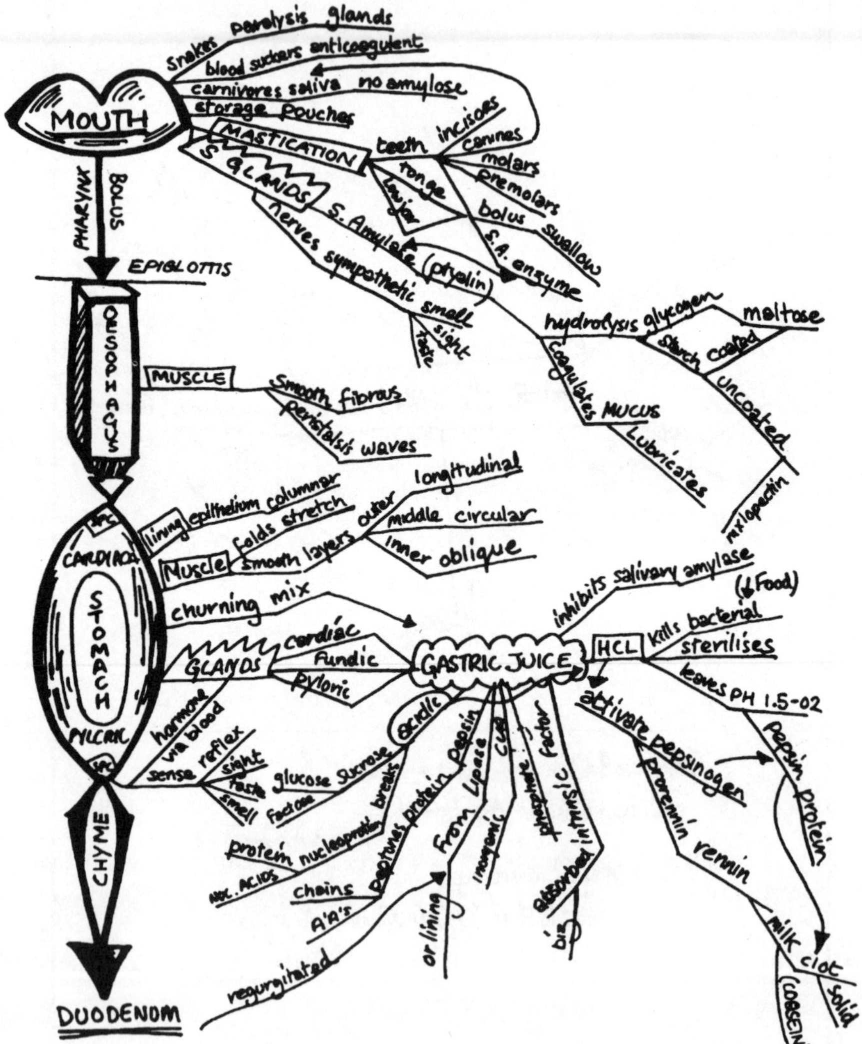

EXAMPLES OF PATTERN NOTES

Example C: a year eleven student's notes

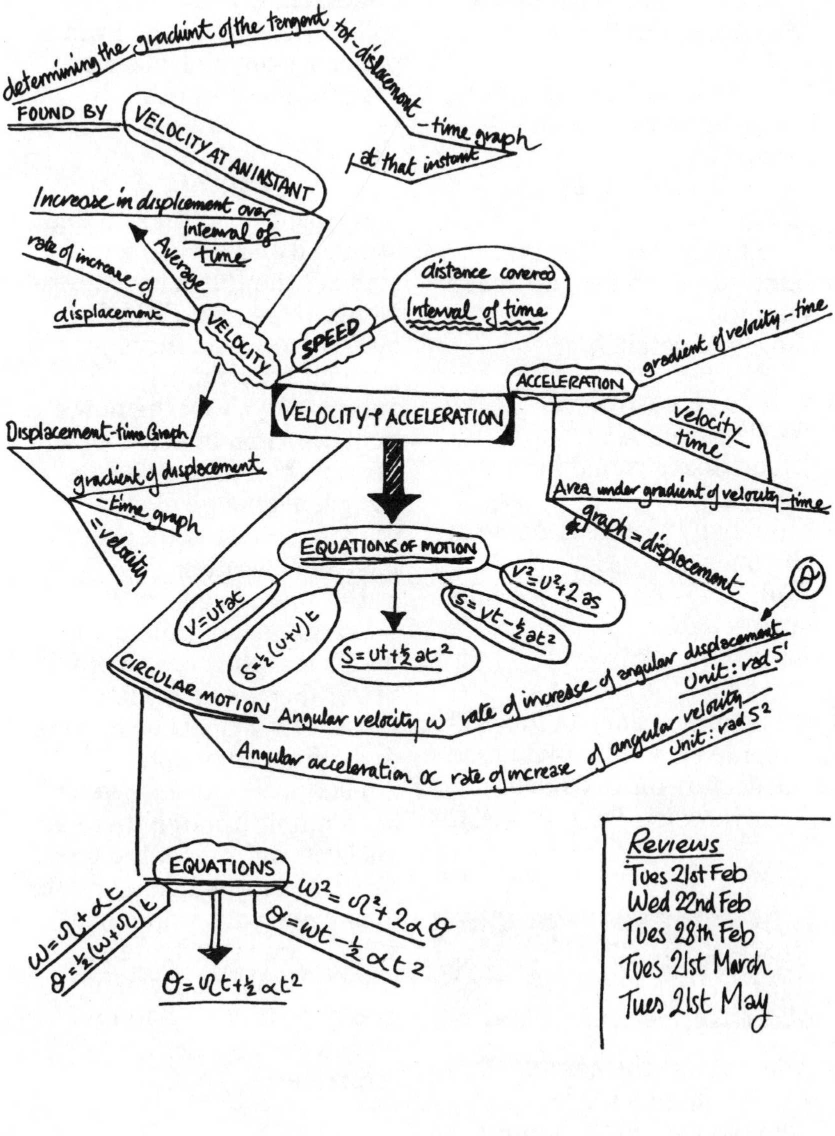

STUDENTS' COMMENTS ON EXAMPLE PATTERN NOTES

Example A

'Not enough information...,
'Should have been printed, not ordinary writing...,
'Too many words on one line, sometimes...,
'Some information added at the end, not in the pattern...,

Example B

'Great shading; like the arrows...,
'Boxes round important things good. ...,
'Too many crossings out...,
'Lines don't change direction enough...,
'Loads of detail...,

Example C

'Well spaced-out...,
'Good boxes round important things...,
'Too many words on some of the lines...,
'This is the only one with the review dates on...*

* The importance of this will become clear when you read the section on Organising Your Revision (pages 25-36).

MORE COMMENTS ON THE EXAMPLE PATTERN NOTES

You can use the comments these students made, and what you yourself thought about the examples, to make your own pattern notes better.

Remember that the brain would prefer to look at a pattern: it finds it easier to understand. Therefore you will learn more easily from a pattern, sketch or diagram than from sentences.

Example A

Some aspects of these notes are good and they follow some of the Rules for Pattern Notes on page 8. (Which ones?) However, there is nothing very visually stimulating about the notes to make them interesting and memorable. There's also a complete change of style at the foot, where sentences have been written.

But there is one really good thing about them, and that is that they are so much better than ordinary linear notes. Why? Because most of the unimportant and unnecessary words haven't been put in (though there are 'the', 'at', 'in', etc. at the foot). Also, the words that all relate to just one part of the main subject are close together — Home, Washing, Drinking, Cooking, 160L — and this makes them easier to remember.

MORE COMMENTS ON EXAMPLE PATTERN NOTES

Example B

- These notes are much more interesting to look at because the pictures make an immediate impression.
- Arrows and shading and the way some words are enclosed make you see immediately which are the most important aspects of the subject.
- However, there is a great deal of detail — more than is really needed — and it would be easier to read if all the words were neatly printed.

Example C

- This is a very clear set of notes, well arranged, and the important topic areas are all highlighted to draw your attention to them. Again though, they would be even better with printed rather than written words.
- This student intends to revise (review) her work, and to do it on carefully planned dates. That is what the box in the bottom right - hand corner is for. There is more about this in Section 9 on Organising Your Revision.
- There is one bad thing though about all the notes — none of them have the date on which they were made. Always put the date on your notes.

FOR YOU TO DO

Practice making some pattern notes. Choose a topic from one of the subjects you are studying and make a set of pattern notes. Before you start, look again at the Rules for Pattern Notes on page 8. Don't make them too detailed or complicated and don't take too long over them — this exercise is just to give you some initial practice.
Then exchange your notes with someone else. Can you both understand each other's? Talk with your partner about how you could improve your own and how they could improve theirs.

SECTION 5 SUMMARY NOTES

Summary Notes are another form of pattern notes. They are closer to linear notes than to pattern notes. (Look again at the examples of pattern notes on pages 9 — 11.) But summary notes are a true pattern and not just chunks of text divided by some space and given some headings. An example of part of a page of summary notes about FUELS on page 7.

RULES FOR SUMMARY NOTES

• Read all the work in your exercise book and any extra information in a text-book.

• Divide topics into the most important points:

Fire

Good fuel

Fossil fuels

Coal

Future Alternatives

• Then expand on each of these headings: What does fire need?

Fire ↗ fuel → Fire oxygen ↘ high temp.

• What makes good fuel?

Good fuel ↗ easy to light/store → slow burn ↘ little ash/smoke.

Where do fuels come from?

Coal buried swamp forests, millions of years ago.

• Then expand on these again: What do we use fuels for and how?

Oil fractional distillation — gas, petrol, etc.

• Expand again: How do these fuels effect the environment?

Coal Coke — slow burn little pollution.

• Make the whole pattern even clearer by using underlining, CAPITALS, arrows, boxing and colour. This makes the points stand out and makes a pattern that's easy to remember.

• Use file paper to make your summary notes.

SUMMARY NOTES

CHECKLIST

• Do they make sense to you?

• Do they really include all the important points?

PRACTICE MAKING SUMMARY NOTES

Look again at For you to Do, on practising making some pattern notes, page 13. Do the same thing for summary notes. Again, exchange with a partner and comment on each other's notes.

SECTION 6 EFFICIENT READING

There are different ways to read a book.

A You can start at page 1 and read through to the end.

B Or look at the Contents list and choose which chapters to read.

C Or flick through the book and read bits here and there.

These are all good ways of getting information from a book. **But for revision you need to know about the most EFFECTIVE AND EFFICIENT WAY OF READING.**

Method A can waste a lot of time. You may not need to know about everything that is in the book.

Method B is better — it will help you to find the topics you need to study but, again you may not need to read the whole chapter.

Method C will give you bits and pieces of information but they may not be the ones which you most need.

• There is another method which is efficient, interesting and produces the results you want.

• It helps you to identify and find the parts of the book that are going to be the most useful to you.

• You will read what you need to read for a particular topic and not waste time on what you don't need.

• Because you read only what is relevant to your subject, it is easier to understand and remember — your mind does not get distracted by information that is not needed at that time.

The method is called <u>**SQ3R**</u>, standing for
Survey,
Question,
Read,
Recall,
Review.

SQ3R

Survey This is to get a general idea of the whole reading piece and to identify the really relevant parts.

Flick over or skim: the contents page; introductions to chapters; headings; diagrams and captions; Final conclusions to chapters: the index.

Question
Ask yourself what questions you want answered by the time you have used the book. These are often the questions that are likely to be in the exam Write down the questions to remind yourself.

Read
Read your chosen pieces, up to a chapter at a time. Look for the chapter's main ideas. These are often n the first and last paragraphs.

Recall
Pick out the main ideas. This is the time to make notes, in your own words. Pattern or summary notes would be best.

Review
Test yourself on your notes to see how much you remember. (More about this later, in the revision section.)

SECTION 6

WRITING ESSAYS

When you learn, you don't only listen, read and make notes. In your course work and in your exams you need to write essays or long answers to questions. There are ways to write good essays.

WHY WRITE ESSAYS?

In an essay you express your own ideas and make your own choice of words. An essay is your own piece of work.

An essay show you, your teacher and your examiner how well you have learned and understood. It identifies your strengths, so that you can be pleased with your achievement. It identifies your weaknesses, so that you will know where you need to improve.

Essay writing for your course work helps you to practice what you will have to do in the exams.

THERE IS A FIVE POINT PLAN WHICH WILL HELP YOU WRITE ESSAYS

1
Understand the task.

2
Assemble the sources you will need.

3
Use the sources efficiently.

4
Make a draft, that is, a plan.

5
Write the essay.

WRITING ESSAYS

LET'S LOOK AT EACH OF THE FIVE POINTS IN MORE DETAIL

1 Understand the task. What exactly is the question asking you to write about? Questions usually have one or more of these key words in them. Pick them out and decide what they mean you must do.

Account	Devise	Outline
Analyse	Discuss	Plan
Apply	Evaluate	Report
Comment	Explain	Review
Compare	Identify	Show
Consider	Illustrate	Specify
Contrast	Indicate	State
Describe	List	Work out

2 Assemble the sources you will need. These can be the items you have been told to read; the notes that you have made yourself; wider written sources, such as books, magazines and newspapers from home or the school or public library; records, tapes, radio or TV programmes. They can also be ideas and opinions, held by you or other people.

3 Use the sources efficiently. Read, using the SQ3R method (page 17). Write any new notes that you need as pattern notes (pages 8 -11) or summary notes (pages 14 - 15). If the source is something to watch or listen to, make brief notes and incorporate them into your pattern or summary notes.

4 Make a draft, that is, a plan.

How will this help?

- It helps you sort out the main points that should be made;
- It makes you think more clearly about your own ideas;
- It may give you more ideas;
- It stops you repeating something you've already said;
- It helps you clarify the order of the essay.

How do you make a draft?

- Ask yourself the key questions that when answered will form the essay;
- If you can't get started on your questions, ask simple ones first such as Who?, What?,Why?, When?, Where?;
- Your draft should be in the form of pattern notes.

5 Write the essay.

- Think first about its structure. There should be three parts:

1 The introduction — your thoughts on what the question means; what approach you are going to take; why you are taking it.

2 The main body of the essay — several paragraphs, each with one main idea; each main idea supported with evidence and examples; the ideas in a good order so that your theme or line of argument can be easily followed by the reader.

3 The conclusion — a summary of the main ideas; the conclusion of the argument; the answer to the question.

- You also need to think about the style — use short sentences; keep the language simple; use good grammar, punctuation and spelling; make clear, useful, labelled diagrams.
- Express your opinions — but don't be dogmatic, don't believe that you must always be right. Be tentative; use words like 'this would suggest' or 'it is possible that' or 'it has been said that'.
- What method will you use to write the essay? You could write it straight through, in a good clear, logical sequence. Or you could write the introduction and the conclusion before

you write the main body. Always read it through when you have finished — to check for and correct any spelling, grammar or punctuation mistakes; to add last-minute information and ideas; to make sure you have quoted sources (from your background reading) accurately.

• Self-assessment — be self-critical; mark your essay (in your mind) before your teacher does; compare your own judgement of the essay with your teacher's. Give yourself a mark out of 10 for:

Effort
Presentation - Organisation
Does it answer the question?
Any original ideas?
Amount of good, relevant points
Is it easy to read and understand?

DISCUSS THESE ASPECTS OF YOUR ESSAY WRITING OR COURSE WORK WITH YOUR TEACHER

SECTION 8 REVISION

WHY SHOULD YOU REVISE?

You would never dream of running a marathon without training first.

So think of revision as your training and your exams as your marathon.

And like training, revision has got to be a continuous process.

You must give yourself time to get better slowly — bit by bit.

Let's see what happens to your chances of remembering something if you don't revise at all.

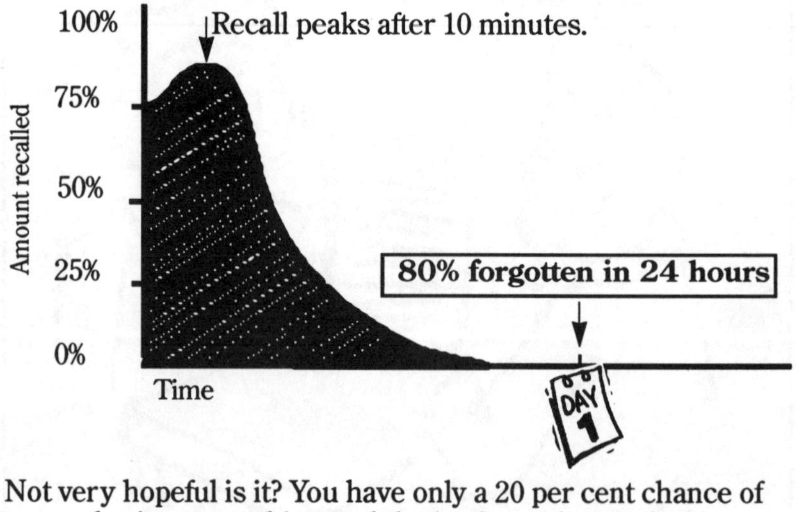

Not very hopeful is it? You have only a 20 per cent chance of remembering everything and that's after only one day!

REVISION

IMPROVING YOUR MEMORY POWER

To get the best out of your brain and remember what you have learned, you should **revise**, or **look at**, or **review** your work at regular intervals, such as,

- the same day you did it;
- then 24 hours later;
- then one week later;
- then one month later, and so on.

Section 9 on Organising Your Revision will show you how to do this.

How properly spaced review can increase your recall over time

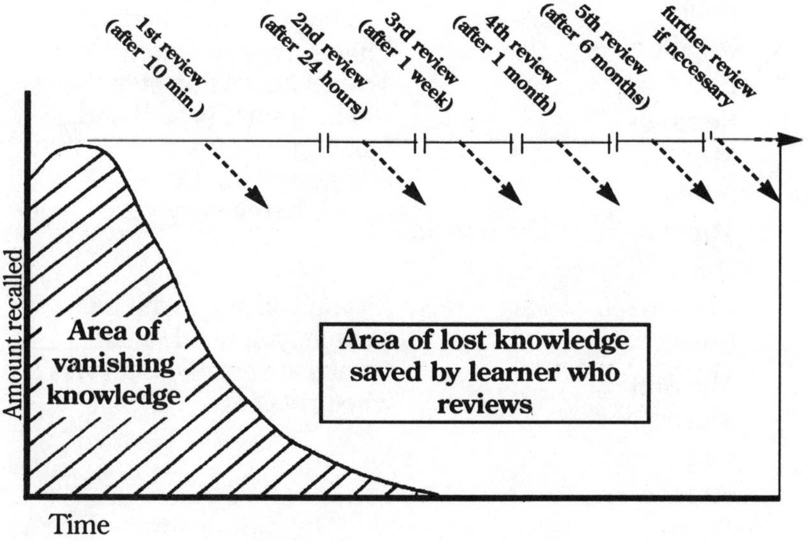

MEMORY TEST

Try this Memory Test

1 Get a pen and piece of paper.

2 Slowly read the list of words below.

3 Cover the words. Don't try to write the words immediately. Leave it for about five minutes. Don't look at the words again during this time. Now write down the ones you can remember.

Cassette
There
Foot
Middle
But
Rescue
More
Apple
There
Quiet
The Queen
But
Message
More
Film
Strange
There
Fright
But
Performance
Ghost

Now I will tell you which ones you may have remembered and which you are likely to have forgoten. *Turn to page 40.*

How can I be right?
It's easy!

You can easily remember words at the beginning of a list or work session, and also at the end, but in the middle you're not very good. Words that appear several times are quite easy to remember as well.

Therefore if you work for several hours non-stop there will be a start (good) and a finish (good) but a lot in the middle will not be remembered very well.

As you will see in the next section, you need to take breaks at sensible intervals when revising.

SECTION 9 ORGANISING YOUR WORK

Organisation is the key to your success. It's knowing when you need to revise something, and knowing what you have already revised yesterday or last month.

STEPS TO REVISION

1

Get yourself a syllabus from your subject teacher. How can you hope to revise the right things if you don't know what you're supposed to have done?

2

Find out what you will be expected to do in your exam. What type of questions will be asked? Will they be essays or multiple choice? How many exam papers are there? How long does each of them last?

3

Each night or whenever you can, choose an area from the syllabus small enough to manage in one evening so that you don't have the usual conversation with teachers:

Teacher — What did you revise last night?

Student — Biology and History.

Teacher — All of it?

Student — No, of course not! I mean I only did 'Breathing and Respiration' and 'The First World War'.

Teacher — That's no good — they are large topics. The syllabus shows you that things are split into small subject areas.

4

Having chosen a small enough piece of work to prepare and revise in one evening, **STOP** and **THINK** about the way you are going to spend your time.

You could:

- Start and not stop until you finish.

- Start and stop half way through. (That shows you chose too much to start with).

- Start but take breaks at sensible intervals.

•See the next page for the best ways of working.

ORGANISING YOUR WORK

- The best way is to keep starting (when memory is good) and finishing (when memory is also good) and cut down on the middle (when things are not so well remembered).
- The best time is 20 minutes work then have a complete rest of about 2-3 minutes.
- The more starts and finishes you have, the better your chances of recall.

The diagram shows you recall when you learn with and without breaks

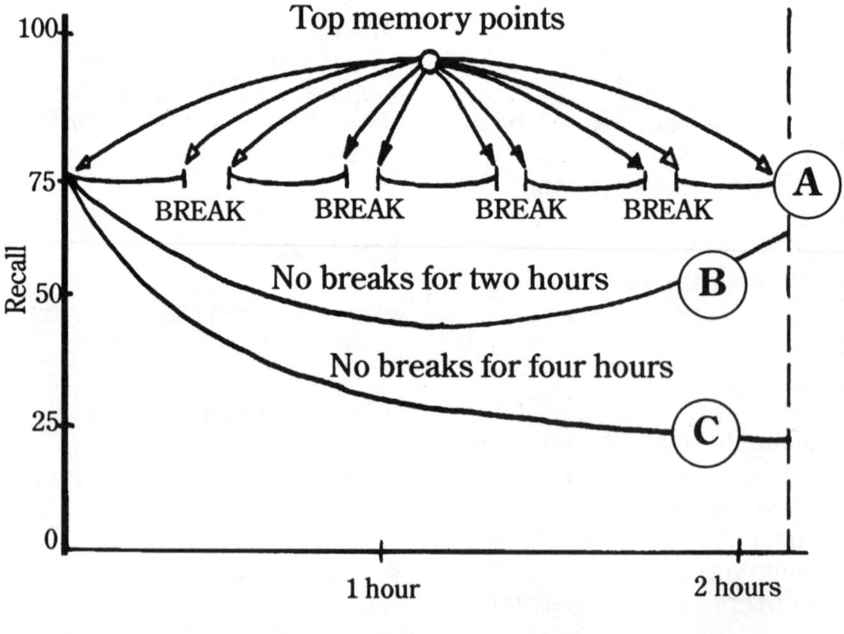

A break = a complete change of activity, minimum of 2 minutes, a maximum of 5.
Suggested work period = 20 minutes

YOUR REVISION PLAN

1 Get a ring binder file.
2 Choose a single topic from the syllabus, for example, The American civil War from the subject History.
3 Read your exercise book notes, text books, your essays, etc., and then make one page (or more if necessary) of Pattern Notes or Summary Notes to cover all the important things you will need to know for the exam.
4 For every set of notes, put at the top the date, the subject and the topic heading. Also put a box in the corner like the one below. This is to show the dates when you are going to revise your notes:

1st revision - the day you begin the system, say, lst January. (1/1)
2nd revision - 24 hours later (2/1, (ie. 2nd January)
3rd revision - one week later (8/1)
4th revision - one month later (1/2)
5th revision - two months later (1/3)
6th revision - three months later (1/4)

1st	Monday	January 1st	
2nd	Tuesday	January 2nd	
3rd	Monday	January 8th	
4st	Monday	February 1st	
5th	Monday	March 1st	
6th	Mondsy	April 1st	

(The actual dates would be slightly different - the important thing to notice is how many weeks and months later you will be doing a revision.)

YOUR REVISION PLAN

DAY 1

1 Take your first set of notes and label it A 1/1 (i.e. it is to be revised on day One, the Ist of January). Put it into your file.

2 Revise A on that day and tick it off.

3 Close the file.

DAY 2

1 Make another set of notes and label it B 2/1 (i.e. to be revised on 2nd Jan.). Put it into the file on top of A.

2 Revise B and tick it off.

3 Turn over B and check if A underneath needs revision. Yes—it needs its 24-hours-later revision.

4 Revise A and tick.

5 Place B back on top of A. Close file.

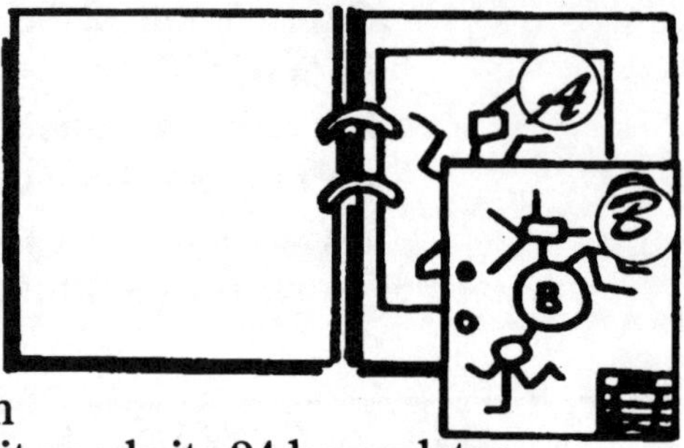

DAY 3

1 Put C 3/1 (ie to be revised on 3rd Jan.) into the file on top of B.

2 Revise C and tick it off.

3 Turn over C and check if B underneath needs revising.Yes — its 24-hours-later revision.

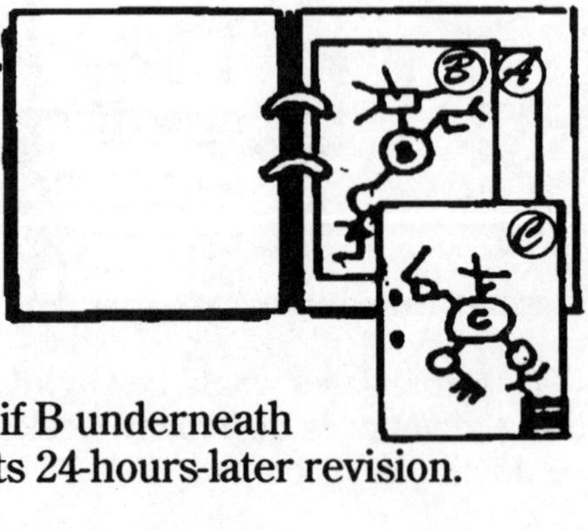

YOUR REVISION PLAN

4 Revise B and tick.
5 Take B out of the file and put it under A.
6 Do you need to revise A? No—its next one is its one-week-later revision, i.e. on 8th Jan.
7 Turn C back over A The order is now CAB.
8 Close file.

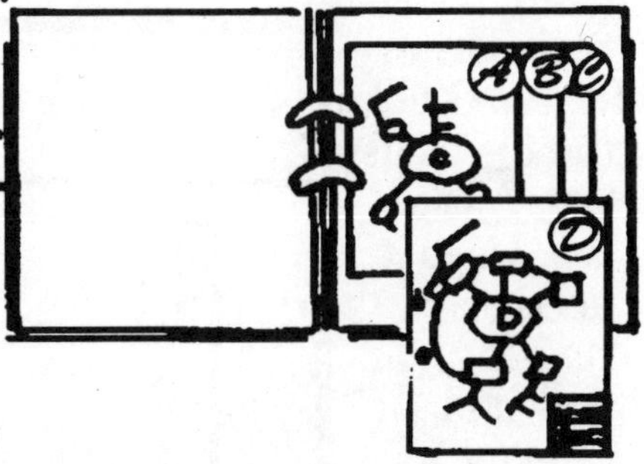

1 Put D 4/1 (i.e. to be revised on 4th Jan.) into the file on top of C.
2 Revise D and tick it off
3 Turn over D and check If C underneath needs revising. Yes—Its 24-hours-later revision.

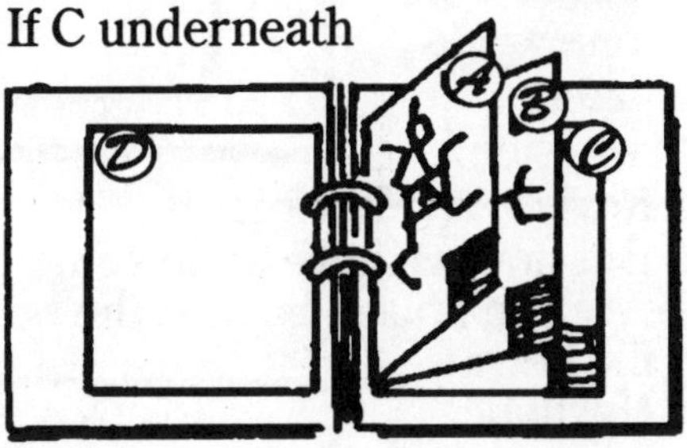

4 Revise C and tick.
5 Take out C and put it under B. A is now on top.
6 Do you need to revise A? No - it is not yet 8th Jan. when its one - week - later revision is due.
7 Turn D back over A. The order is now DABC.
8 Close file.

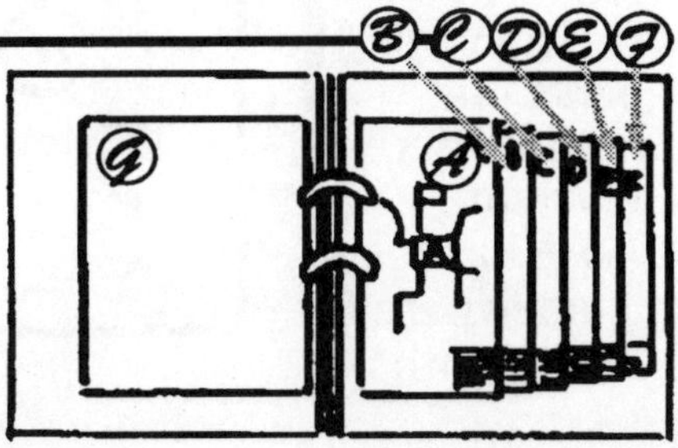

1 Continue this method of revising and filing.
2 On Day Seven the order will be GABCDEF.

YOUR REVISION PLAN

1 Put H 8/1 in the file. revise and tick off

2 Turn over H and look at G Does it need revising? Yes — its 24-hours-later revision.

3 Revise G,tick it off, and put it at the back of the file as usual.

4 Now A is on top. Does it need revising? Yes now it is time for its one week-later revision.

5 Revise A and tick it off

6 But now we have to do something different.

- We can't put A back at the bottom of the file because H will be going there to wait for its one-week-later revision.
- A's next revision will be its one month-later revision.
- So A has to go somewhere for one month.

YOUR REVISION PLAN

• Answer? Get yourself a file divider.
7 Put the divider underneath G.
8 Put A at the back, under the divider.
The order is now:

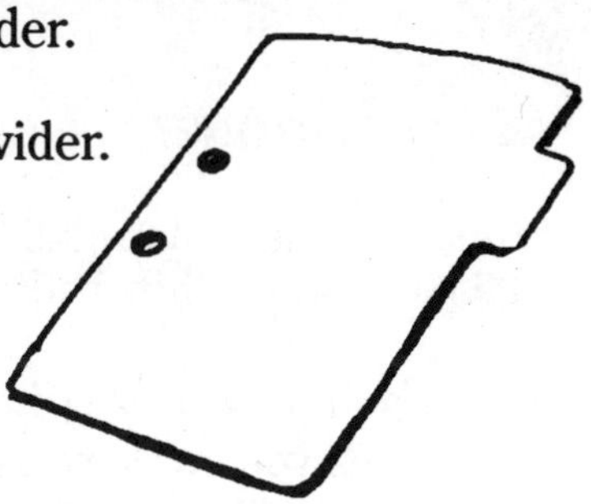

	DIVIDER	
H-BCDEFG	D I V I D E R	A 1 MONTH

DAY 9

1 Follow the system, revising H and putting it underneath G.
2 B Will then be on top and after its revision it will go, like A, to the back under the divider to wait for its one month - later revision.

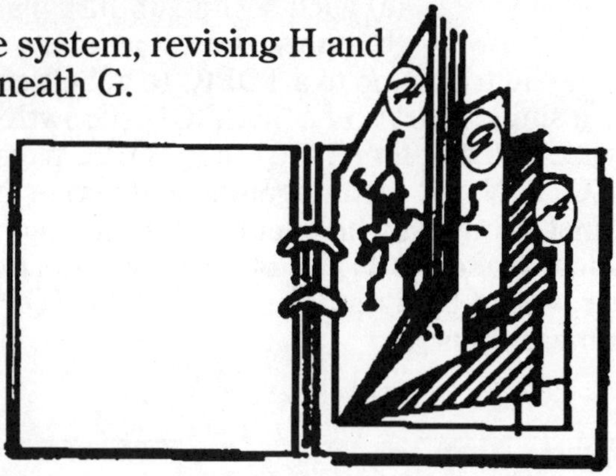

3 The order is now:

	DIVIDER	
I-CDEFGH	D I V I D E R	AB 1 MONTH

This will be the pattern of organisation for your 'floating file' revision.
Be methodical.
Stick to the routine.
You will soon become used to it.

YOUR REVISION PLAN

ANY QUESTIONS?

Students in school use this revision plan, and these are some of the questions they had.

1 *Q. Can I only do one piece of revision every night?*

A. No. If you do more, you will have more than one piece of paper but they will all share the same dates and therefore they can be revised on the same evening and moved about together.

2 *Q. I'll soon have too much paper in my file!*

A . After one month, as long as you revise

(a) each section of the syllabus in order and

(b) one section at a time,

then you will come to a TOPIC (e.g. Settlement), which would be a single TOPIC of a SECTION (Growth of USA) of the syllabus. Look for all the other TOPIC pages to do with this SECTION, put them together, and revise them all by transferring the whole lot of information onto one pattern. As below, make the TITLE of the new pattern a general heading (Growth of USA) and then set out the TOPICS around it as sub-headings.

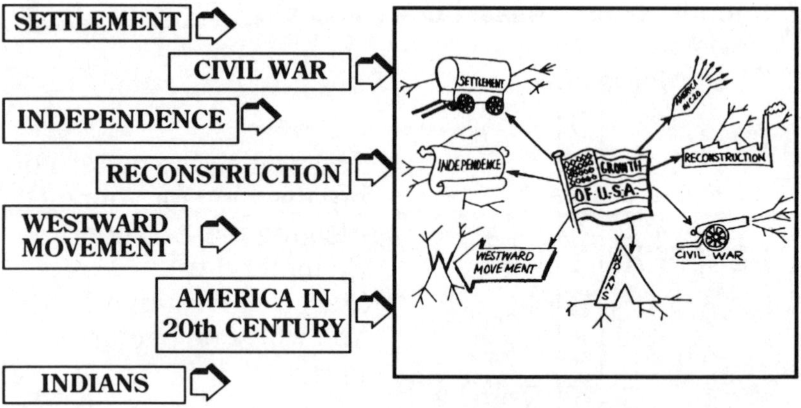

3 Q. I'm not that good. It seems I'll have to revise every single day. That will not be possible.

A. True. A piece of paper has to be put in your file every day but it can be blank as long as it's got all the dates on it. This will keep the papers spread out properly.

You will probably have to revise something each night because things keep turning up, but how long will this take? (2-3 minutes?)

N.B. Never bring this revision file to school – keep it safely at home

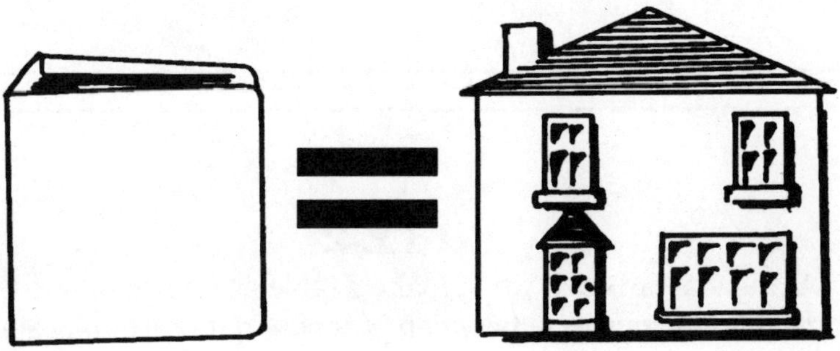

SOME MORE REVISION RULES

Some more revision rules

There are two types of work you usually do at home. One is called 'Keeping out of trouble' work. This is work you have been asked to do by a teacher and involves giving it in, sometimes tomorrow or more usually in a couple of days. If you don't, it's a report or detention. The other is called 'Selfish' work, which is work you are doing for yourself, like revision.

RULE 1

Do your 'Keeping out of trouble work' first — only revise when you have done all your usual day-to-day homework.

All done? Now you can do your 'Selfish' work or revision.

RULE 2

At the start of each week make a table as shown opposite. Divide up your time between 'Keeping out of trouble' and 'Selfish' time

SOME MORE REVISION RULES

KEEPING OUT OF TROUBLE TIME	SELFISH (REVISION) TIME
During the course of the school year you can tell roughly how much work you will be set in one week. Plan and do this work first — it may take about 7 hours out of the week. You should allow $1\frac{1}{2}$ hours a day (including Saturdays and Sundays) for all your school work — including 'Keeping out of trouble' work.	If you *usually* need 7 hours or more to keep out of trouble, you will be left with only about $3\frac{1}{2}$ hours of revision. Make a list of $3\frac{1}{2}$ hours worth of revision at the beginning of the week from the subject syllabuses. Tick off each subject as you do it. For example: **1** 'The cell' — time approx. $\frac{1}{2}$ hour **2** 'First World War, Sarajevo' — $\frac{3}{4}$ hour **3** etc. **4** etc. **5** etc.

When you have completed your floating file system, and organised your 'Keeping out of trouble'/ 'Selfish' time, you will have a real method of revision.

START NOW!

BE ORGANISED!

NOW YOU ARE ORGANISED, WHAT NEXT?

Now you know *what* to revise and *how often* to do it, you need to know *how best* to do it.

Revision should be active and it should be in three stages:

1 Test

2 Check

3 Retest

1 Test

- Look through your chosen pattern notes.
- Think carefully about each word and how it connects with the other words.
- Without looking, try to draw out the pattern again.

2 Check did one of these things happen?

- *You got all the words right and the pattern was the same.* (Very unlikely but congratulations!) There's no need to do anything until next revision time (remember?) same day, 24 hours later, one week later etc.

- *You got all the words right but the pattern was different.* This means, your brain is thinking about these notes in a new pattern. So throw the first pattern away and file away your new pattern for your next revision.

- *You got some of the words wrong and the pattern was different.* You need help with the wrong words. Using your new pattern, write on the words you forgot in a different colour, or box, or underline them. Throw away your old pattern and file away the new one for your next revision.

3 Retest

- At your next revision time look carefully at your pattern again, reminding yourself particularly of the words you didn't know last time.

- Try to draw out the pattern again without looking.

SECTION 10 ON THE EXAM DAY

If you have learned to take short, accurate, fact-packed notes –

If you have asked for extra syllabuses –

If you have started your revision in time and you have been very organised –

You will do better than you expect.

ON THE NIGHT BEFORE

1 Get a good night's sleep.

2 Get everything ready before you go to bed:
PEN, AT LEAST TWO BIROS, PENCILS, RUBBERS, RULERS, CALCULATORS, ETC.

ON THE DAY

1 Get up early so you can arrive at school or your exam centre with plenty of time to spare.

2 Only talk, with your friends, about what you **DO** know and not what you **DON'T** know just before the exam.

3 Make sure you have enough time to complete the required number of questions. Check with the clock to see that you divide your time equally between all the questions. Keep an eye on the clock. If time runs out and a question is unfinished, **LEAVE IT** and **GO ON** to the next one.

3 Before you start any question, **READ IT VERY CAREFULLY**, making sure that you understand it. Only answer **WHAT THE QUESTION ASKS YOU.** You won't get marks for even the most brilliant answer if it is not what the question asks for.

ON THE EXAM DAY

6 If you find time is running out on a question, write only brief notes. You will still get some marks for them.

7 Write as neatly as you possibly can under pressure. You won't get marks for an answer the examiner can't read.

8 Leave enough time to read through ALL your answers at the end. You may be able to correct one or two mistakes and so gain an extra mark or two. It's worth it.

If you are doing a paper which only has essays:

1 AFTER CHOOSING YOUR QUESTIONS
Write a plan for all your answers, one after another, at the start of the exam when you are at your LEAST TIRED. The plans (working out what you are going to write) are the most tiring.

2 Then, all that's left is the time-consuming task of turning your plans into essays that can be marked.

GOOD LUCK !
BUT IF YOU FOLLOWED
EVERYTHING IN THIS BOOK,
LUCK,
GOOD OR BAD,–
WON'T COME INTO IT!

SOMETHING EXTRA

Did you read pages 16 — 17 on Reading ?
Here is a short test — It's simple and it won't take long,

<u>Answer all questions.</u>

1 Work out 9 x 7– 9.
2 Write your name backwards.
3 Write down the months of the year that have an R in them.
4 Write down all the sports you play.
5 What's your favourite food? No need to write it down.
6 Write down all the names you can of all the planets.
7 Work out the answer to 6 + 2 - 4.
8 What school do you go to?
9 What's your favourite colour?
10 What's your favourite book?
11 Who's your favourite author?
12 Have you any pets ? Draw any pets you have.
13 What do you think of all the questions in the test so far?
14 Ignore all the questions that come before this question. If you haven't, then carry out the instruction in question 15. Smile, because you have been tricked. Don't read so inefficiently again. You cannot afford the waste of time.
15 Re–read the Survey section of the SQ3R reading method.

ANSWERS

ANSWER TO MEMORY TEST ON PAGE 24

You should have remembered the repeated words:-

There
But
More

You may have remembered words from the beginning:

Cassette
Foot
Middle

You should have remembered words from the end:

Fright
Performance
Ghost

You definitely remembered The Queen. Anything that is outstandingly different is memorable!